We believe in a future where a collec

applying the science of reading throu

leader preparation, classroom application, and community engagement will elevate and transform every community, every nation, through the power of literacy.

MW01710254

Rationale for Promoting a Common Definition of the Science of Reading

Although the scientific evidence base for effective reading has existed for decades, the term "the science of reading" has gained traction in the last few years, potentially leading to misunderstandings. As a result, we believe that a common definition is useful for the field.

A Common Definition Will:

- Support educators and parents as they discern what is and what is not in alignment with the science of reading.
- Assist people in becoming informed and wiser consumers of instructional materials, professional development, and resources.
- Impact publishers' and policy makers' decisions as they develop materials and policy guidelines.
- Guide people in the true educational transformation needed for sustainable change to effective practice.
- Unify the effort of all stakeholders on behalf of students to ensure the advancement of educational equity.

The Definition

The **science of reading** is a vast, interdisciplinary body of *scientifically-based** research about reading and issues related to reading and writing.

This research has been conducted over the last five decades across the world, and it is derived from thousands of studies conducted in multiple languages. The science of reading has culminated in a preponderance of evidence to inform how proficient reading and writing develop; why some have difficulty; and how we can most effectively assess and teach and, therefore, improve student outcomes through prevention of and intervention for reading difficulties.

* See the chart on page 11 for a better understanding of what is meant by scientifically-based research

The Science of Reading is Derived From Researchers in Multiple Fields:

- Cognitive Psychology
- Communication Sciences
- Developmental Psychology
- Education
- Special Education
- Implementation Science
- Linguistics
- Neuroscience
- School Psychology

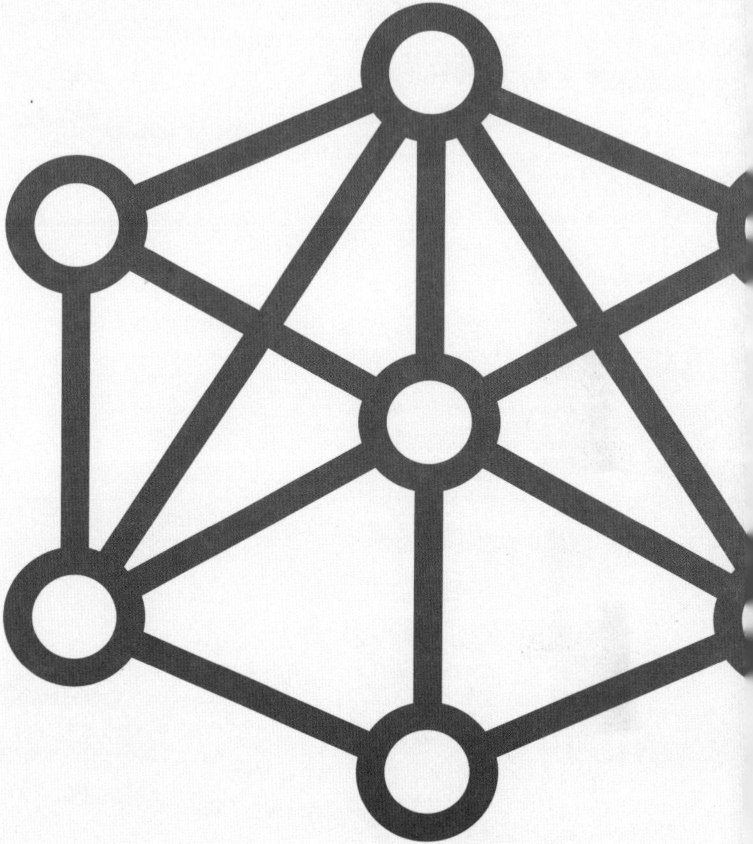

What the Science of Reading is **NOT**

- an ideology or philosophy
- a fad, trend, new idea, or pendulum swing
- a political agenda
- a one-size-fits-all approach
- a program of instruction
- a single, specific component of instruction, such as phonics

Findings From *Scientifically-Based Research* Are Best Able To Inform Effective Instruction

The type of question being asked determines the method/approach of research. While questions about the causal relationships between instruction and student outcomes that comprise the science of reading are best answered with experimental or quasi-experimental research designs, other methodologies (e.g., qualitative studies, brain imaging studies, correlational studies, observational studies, meta-analyses) are useful when the research questions are not seeking to address causal claims.

> *"Teachers can benefit by understanding two things about research and causal inferences. The first is the simple (but sometimes obscured) fact that statements about best instructional practices are statements that contain causal claims. These statements claim that one type of method or practice causes superior educational outcomes. Second, teachers must understand how the logic of the experimental method provides the critical support for making causal inferences."*

Stanovich, P. J. & Stanovich, K. E. (2003). *Using research and reason in education: How teachers can use scientifically based research to make curricular & instructional decisions*. National Institute of Child Health and Human Development; Department of Education; and Department of Health and Human Services.

* Scientifically-based research includes the components described in the table below.

REQUIRED COMPONENTS	DEFINITIONS	WHY IMPORTANT
Study design that is experimental or quasi-experimental. These designs specifically answer questions about why individuals have difficulty learning to read and write, as well as which practices are effective.	**Experimental** design features one or more experimental groups and at least one comparison group. Participants are randomly assigned to groups. **Quasi-experimental** design does not utilize random assignment. Participants are sometimes compared to groups with similar profiles.	Experimental and quasi-experimental designs allow researchers to determine if a particular variable being studied is the reason for improved outcomes. Random assignment, recognized as the gold standard, provides a clearer link between cause and effect because it helps control the effects of variables other than the experimental treatment. This allows for greater confidence that the treatment is what led to improved outcomes.
Detailed description of study methods and population for replication, generalizability, or refinement of findings.	To have confidence in findings, a convergence of evidence is needed. Detailed descriptions regarding design, participants, settings, instructional practices, measurements, and outcomes must be provided to replicate the study (i.e., conduct another study in a similar manner). Generalizability is the extent to which the findings of a study would be expected in real-world contexts.	It is important to show that scientific findings are unbiased and to determine for whom and under what conditions positive outcomes are produced. Replication is what leads to a large body of studies with similar results so that we can: **a.** Conclude findings are consistent (e.g., "on the right road") **b**. Conclude findings are not consistent (e.g., more research needed) **c.** Discover new questions to be studied Clear descriptions of the context in which the study was conducted, the resources involved, and the participants allow readers to evaluate whether similar findings might be expected in their situations.
Publication in a **peer-reviewed** (refereed) journal.	**Peer-reviewed** journals provide a rigorous review by multiple independent scientists with relevant expertise.	**Peer review** is a "quality check" prior to publication to ensure the study and its outcomes were designed, executed, and described properly. It provides integrity to the body of studies that make up the science of reading.

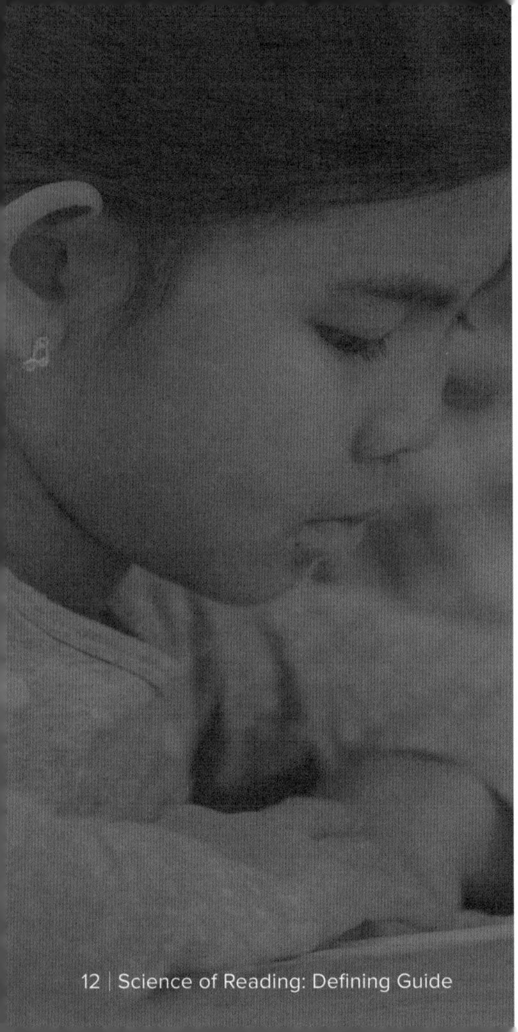

Reading Processes, Reading Development, and Instructional Practices: An Introduction

> *Research in reading should follow the norms of science. Each researcher must try to learn from the work of those who preceded him and to add to a unified body of knowledge.*
>
> (Chall, 1967, p. 314).

As with any body of knowledge derived from science, the body of scientifically-based reading research builds and advances over time. It has provided us with information about reading development, reading processes, and reading instruction.

Interdisciplinary findings converge to refine and confirm existing findings, adding strength and validity. In contrast to basing reading instruction on theories or philosophies, knowledge of the large body of scientific research called the science of reading allows practitioners to select and implement practices about reading that will be the most effective for the most students.

Reading Processes: What the Science of Reading Reveals About How Reading is Processed in the Brain

In recent years, our knowledge of how the brain acquires the skill of reading has evolved. We now have a deeper understanding of how the brain processes multiple sources of information while reading. Brain researchers have identified areas and networks of the brain involved in processing print, speech sounds, language, and meaning.

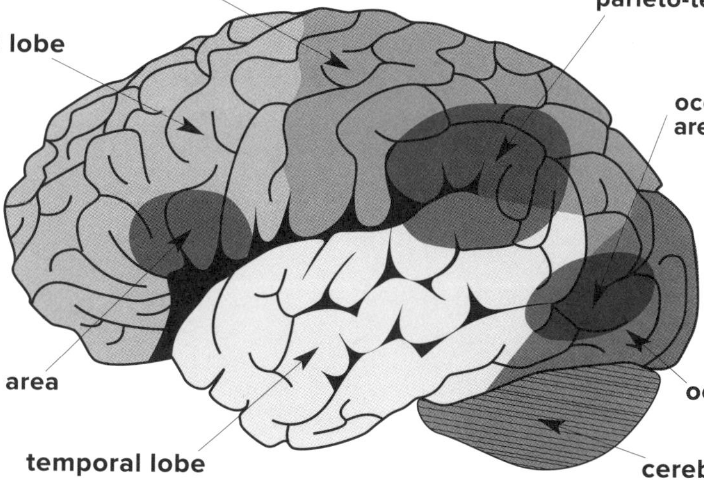

© CORE, Teaching Reading Sourcebook, 3nd Ed., 2018, Arena Press, page 4.

Since neural connections required for reading do not exist between these areas in the pre-literate brain, efficient pathways are built with explicit instruction and deliberate practice. This instruction has a significant influence on building these networks, over and above “immersion” and instruction that is not explicit.

Educators who are knowledgeable about the necessary connections between the pronunciation of the spoken word, the sequence of letters in the printed word, and the meaning of the word, can implement reading instruction and assessment that promotes the level of automatic word recognition that is necessary for deep processing of the meaning of texts.

TO LEARN MORE:

Watch the first 15 minutes of this video on how the brain learns to read:
http://bit.ly/HowtheBrainLearnstoRead

See pages 21-32 in the link below for an illustration of a time-lapse of fMRI brain images representing the language processes that operate during both reading and speaking.
http://bit.ly/ScienceofReadingPrimer1

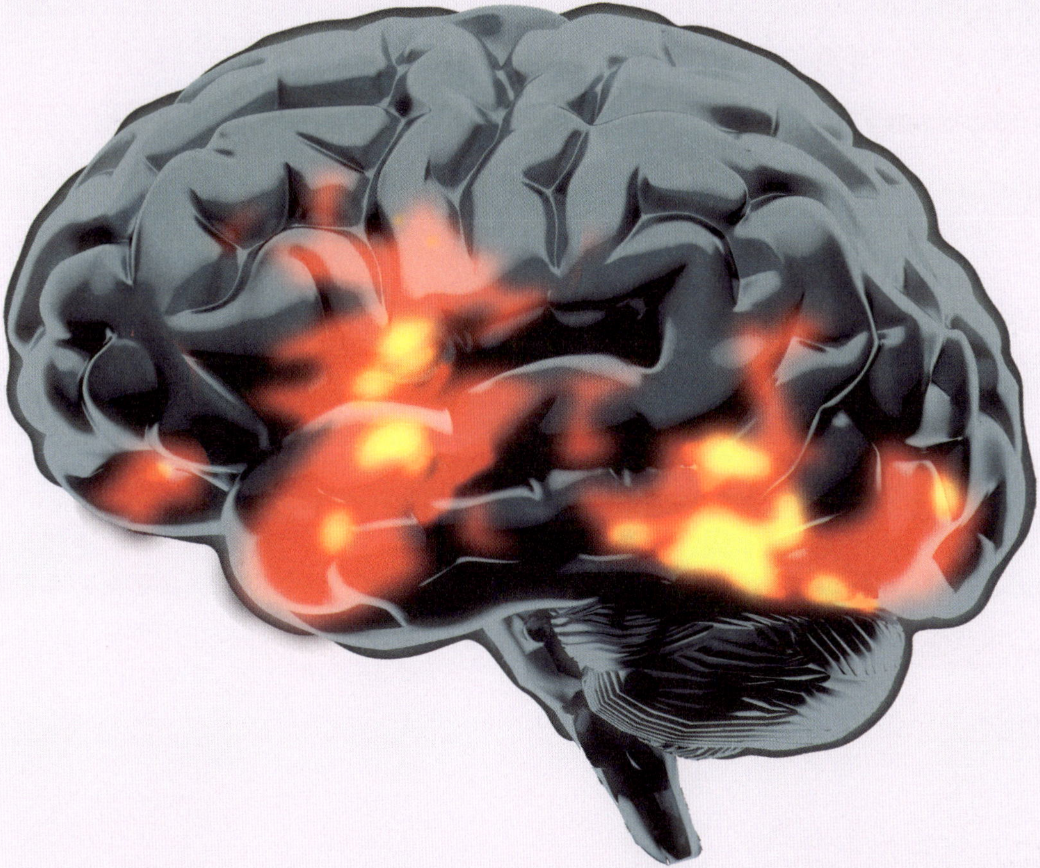

Reading Development: What the Science of Reading Discovered About How Skillful Reading Develops

To understand how a student develops into a skillful reader (i.e., a fluent reader who can comprehend text), we look toward two theoretical frameworks aligned with science. We encourage all stakeholders to familiarize themselves with these frameworks as they should be used to inform reading assessment and instruction.

SIMPLE VIEW OF READING

The Simple View of Reading has been empirically validated by over 150 scientific studies. It shows us that reading comprehension is not the sum, but the product of two components - word recognition and language comprehension - such that if either one is weak, reading comprehension is diminished. No amount of skill in one component can compensate for a lack of skill in the other. While it is a simple view of a developmental process, skilled reading development is NOT simplistic. For a more in-depth understanding of the subcomponents within word recognition (WR) and language comprehension (LC), we turn next to Scarborough's Reading Rope.

Gough, P. B., & Tunmer, W. E. (1986). Decoding, reading, and reading disability. *Remedial and Special Education*, 7, 6-10.

SCARBOROUGH'S READING ROPE

Scarborough's Rope is a visual metaphor for the development of skills over time (represented by the strands of the rope) that lead to skilled reading.

Scarborough, H. S. (2001). Connecting early language and literacy to later reading (dis)abilities: Evidence, theory, and practice. In S. Neuman & D. Dickinson (Eds.), *Handbook for research in early literacy,* (pp. 97-110). Guilford.

Language Comprehension

Background Knowledge
(facts, concepts, etc.)

Vocabulary
(breadth, precision, links, etc.)

Language Structures
(syntax, semantics, etc.)

Verbal Reasoning
(inference, metaphor, etc.)

Literacy Knowledge
(print concepts, genres, etc.)

Word Recognition

Phonological Awareness
(syllables, phonemes, etc.)

Decoding
(alphabetic principle, spelling-sound correspondences)

Sight Recognition
(of familiar words)

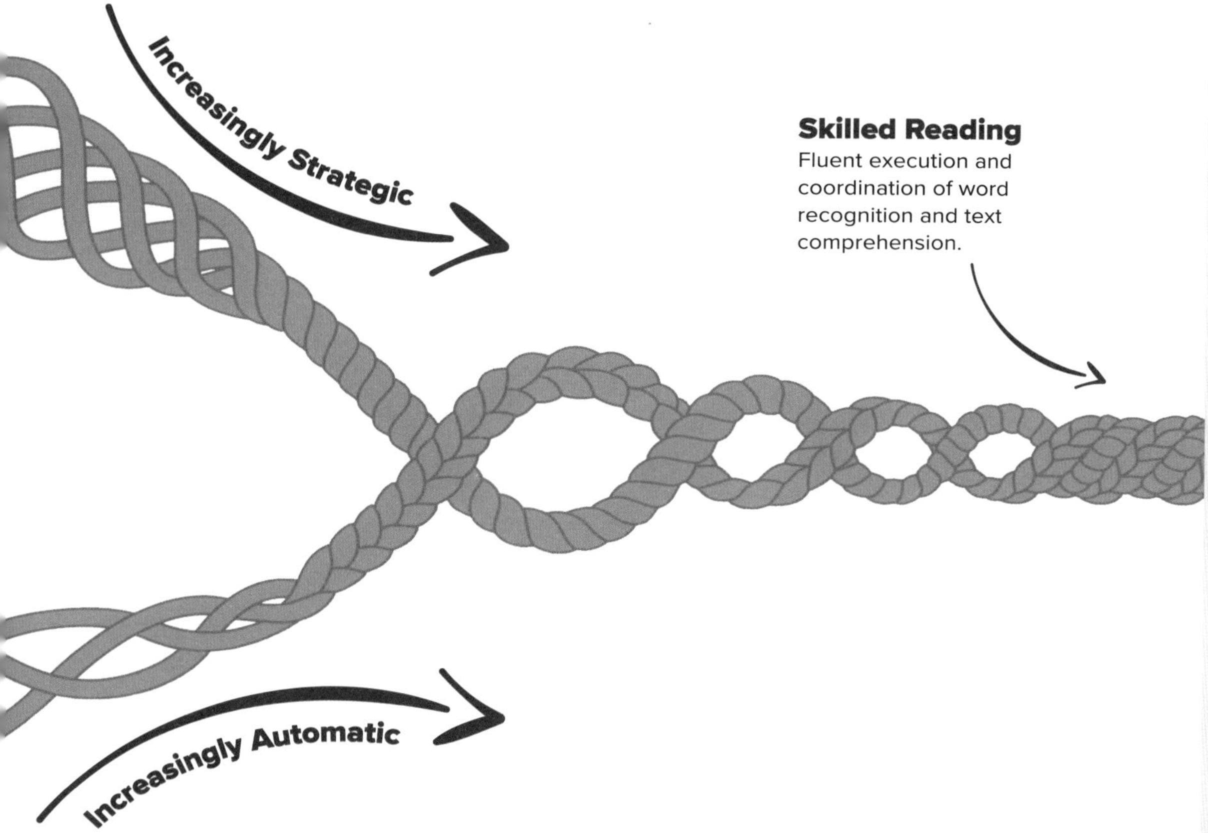

The Reading Rope (Scarborough, 2001)

Patterns of Reading Skills Derived From the Science of Reading Inform Instruction for *All* Learners

The Simple View of Reading allows us to recognize patterns of reading skills in both word recognition/decoding and language comprehension. Knowing where learners fall on the continuum of reading patterns depicted on the next page provides insight into the reasons for the reading difficulty and where to focus instruction.

Based on the Simple View of Reading, each of the three patterns in which there is a weak area will result in diminished reading comprehension. Universal screening and diagnostic assessment data must inform student strengths and needs that then become the focus of instruction and intervention.

See Gough, P. B., & Tunmer, W. E. (1986). Decoding, reading, and reading disability. *Remedial and Special Education*, 7, 6-10.

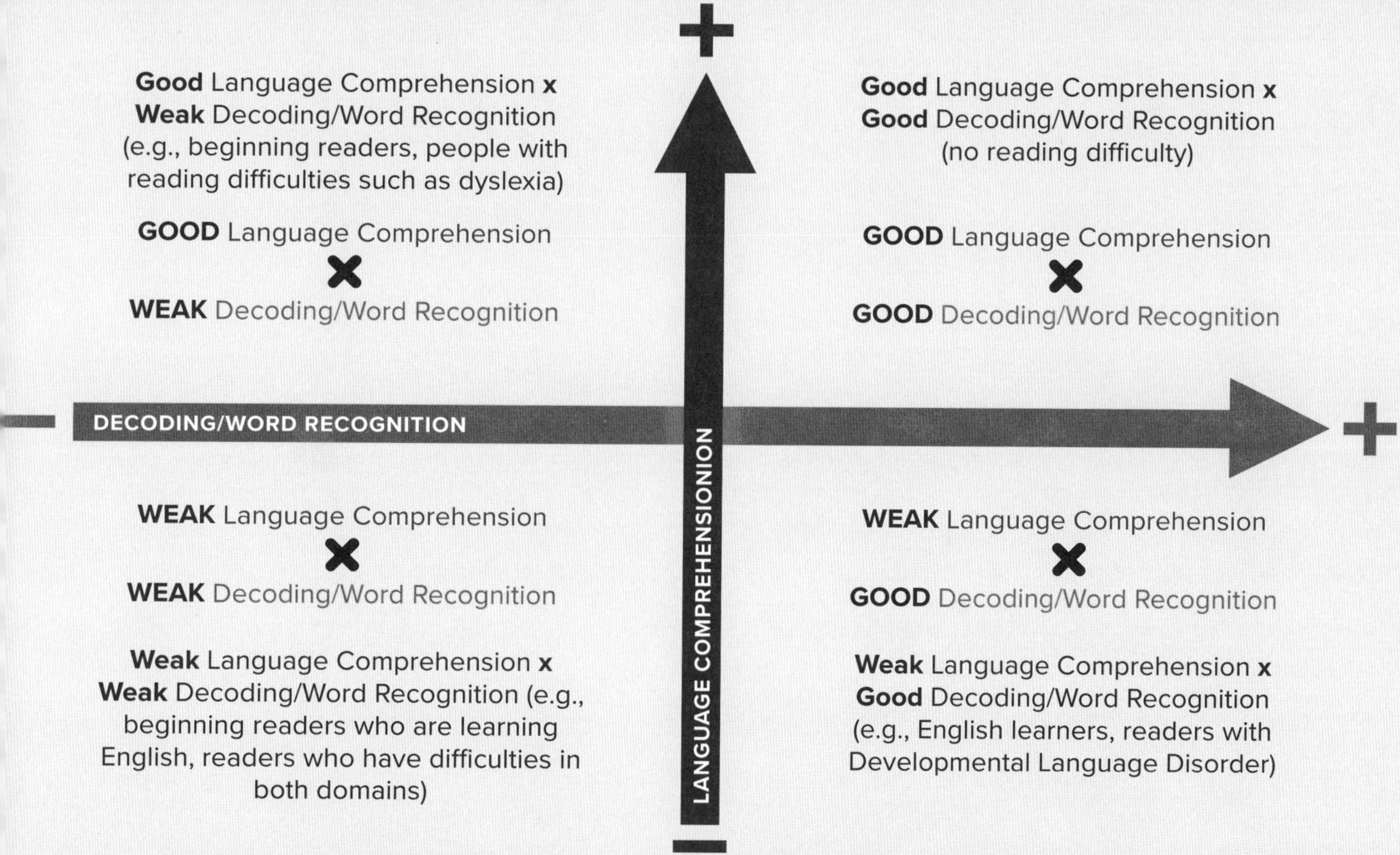

Good Language Comprehension **x**
Weak Decoding/Word Recognition
(e.g., beginning readers, people with reading difficulties such as dyslexia)
GOOD Language Comprehension
WEAK Decoding/Word Recognition
Good Language Comprehension **x**
Good Decoding/Word Recognition
(no reading difficulty)
GOOD Language Comprehension
GOOD Decoding/Word Recognition
DECODING/WORD RECOGNITION
LANGUAGE COMPREHENSIONION
WEAK Language Comprehension
WEAK Decoding/Word Recognition
Weak Language Comprehension **x**
Weak Decoding/Word Recognition (e.g., beginning readers who are learning English, readers who have difficulties in both domains)
WEAK Language Comprehension
GOOD Decoding/Word Recognition
Weak Language Comprehension **x**
Good Decoding/Word Recognition
(e.g., English learners, readers with Developmental Language Disorder)

Instructional Practices Aligned With the Science of Reading: Word Recognition

The following is a *sampling* of instructional practices for word recognition. It is not an exhaustive list.

Examples of instructional practices aligned with findings from the scientific evidence base:

- Phonemic awareness and letter instruction: Instruction in the identification of phonemes in spoken words and how they link to letters.
- Explicit and systematic instruction in how to decode (read) and encode (spell) words, including word part analysis (e.g., syllables, morphemes).
- Connected text reading to build reading accuracy automaticity, fluency, and comprehension.

Examples of instructional practices NOT supported by scientific evidence:

- Emphasis on larger units of speech (syllables, rhyme, onset-rime) rather than individual phonemes.
- Implicit and incidental instruction in word reading, visual memorization of whole words, guessing from context, and picture cues.
- Emphasis on speed or words per minute over accuracy when reading texts (practiced with reading of patterned texts or sustained silent reading for all students).

Instructional Practices Aligned With the Science of Reading: Language Comprehension

The following is a *sampling* of instructional practices for language comprehension. It is not an exhaustive list.

Examples of instructional practices aligned with findings from the scientific evidence base:

- Read-alouds from a variety of complex texts to build knowledge and vocabulary.
- Robust conversations to develop students' academic language (e.g., narrative and inferential language).
- Explicit instruction in grammatical structures and academic vocabulary within the context of other reading activities.

Examples of instructional practices NOT supported by scientific evidence:

- Read-alouds from leveled texts that students will be reading so that text is not sufficiently complex.
- A lack of explicit instruction of morphology, memorization of isolated words and definitions out of context, and a lack of strategic and intentional instruction.
- Implicit instruction of grammatical structures.

The Science of Reading Includes Learners with Linguistic Differences

Educators supporting students with linguistic differences such as multilingual learners (MLLs), English learners (ELs), and speakers of English language variations can rely on the science of reading and the conceptual frameworks highlighted in this guide. These students benefit from the practices derived from the science of reading. All proficient readers must master the same concepts in order to learn to read. However, it is important to provide students with linguistic differences a focused attention on oral language development.

> *"Both English literacy and English oral language proficiency must be priorities if these students are to have adequate and equitable opportunities for success in school and beyond."*

(Goldenberg, 2020: bit.ly/Goldenberg2020RdgWarsRdgScienceEngLearners).

> *"The linguistic differences that children bring with them to school should be viewed positively in classrooms and used as strengths to leverage performance in literacy."*

B Gatlin-Nash, L Johnson, R Lee-James. International Dyslexia Association: *Perspectives on Language and Literacy*, 28-35, 2020.

> *"ELs benefit from reading instruction that includes phonemic awareness, phonics, fluency, vocabulary, and text comprehension. Adjustments are necessary, however. One of the major adjustments includes a focus on oral language proficiency, which is often overlooked during instruction."*

(Cárdenas-Hagan, 2020, p. 38: https://bit.ly/Cardenas-HaganText).

Additional Resources:

ASHA Phonemic Inventories and Cultural and Linguistic Information Across Languages:
https://www.asha.org/Practice/multicultural/Phono/

Gatlin-Nash, Johnson, & Lee-James (2020):
http://www.onlinedigeditions.com/publication/?m=13959&i=671218&p=3&pp=1&ver=html5

Seidenberg & Washington (2021):
https://www.aft.org/ae/summer2021/washington_seidenberg

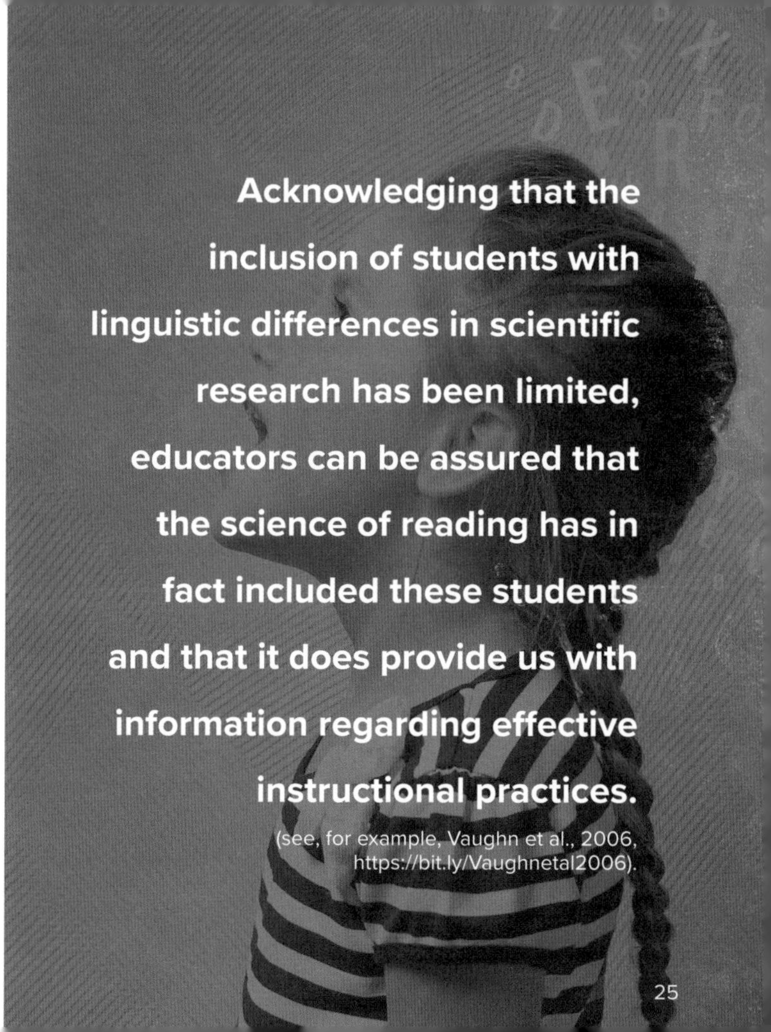

Acknowledging that the inclusion of students with linguistic differences in scientific research has been limited, educators can be assured that the science of reading has in fact included these students and that it does provide us with information regarding effective instructional practices.

(see, for example, Vaughn et al., 2006, https://bit.ly/Vaughnetal2006).

MTSS: A Framework to Improve Reading Outcomes Through Prevention and Intervention

Multi-Tiered Systems of Support (MTSS) is a school-wide framework for implementing effective instruction. MTSS involves efficiently targeting instruction to student needs based on universal screening and diagnostic assessments.

School and district teams use assessments in a data-based, decision-making process to build a system of increasingly intensive instructional supports that are customized to fit the needs of the students. Simultaneously, schools must also assess their human and instructional resources to ensure that those needs are met.

MTSS does not involve prescriptive practices to be rigidly implemented by tiers or levels of assignment. Nor is it adding to current, ineffective practices for the sake of innovation. It is a comprehensive system whereby ineffective practices are strategically abandoned and proven practices are prioritized.

By focusing first on meeting the needs of the vast majority of students through an effective system of universal, core instruction, more intensive and specialized resources such as funding, instructional minutes, and educator capacity are available to serve students with complex reading needs.

Rather than waiting for students to fall behind before providing reading support, the MTSS model provides the early identification of risk and immediate instructional response that improves student outcomes through prevention of and intervention for reading difficulties.

Calls to Action for All Stakeholders

We call on **educators** to embrace opportunities to learn about the science of reading, reflect upon their practice, and challenge approaches to reading instruction that are not aligned with the scientific evidence.

We call on **district and school administrators, school boards, and school committees** to prioritize professional development on the science of reading for themselves and for educators and to provide the necessary support (e.g., coaching) to adopt evidence-aligned assessments, resources, and instructional practices.

We call on **state departments of education** to collaborate with experts in the science of reading to design responsible rollouts of integrated initiatives based on the findings from the science of reading and to prioritize leadership preparation to support teacher implementation of evidence aligned practices (e.g., educator standards, licensing exams).

We call on **schools of education** to align coursework with the science of reading and to foster interdisciplinary collaboration between professors of education and professors of cognitive psychology, neuroscience, speech and language studies, linguistics, and related fields.

We call on **pediatricians** to prioritize the screening of early speech and language developmental milestones to identify red flags for future reading difficulties.

We call on **curriculum publishers and professional learning providers** to create and promote products that are aligned with the science of reading, and to eliminate non-aligned products from their offerings.

We call on **federal agencies and private foundations** to continue to fund research on issues and questions critical to better understanding reading development, reading difficulties, and the most effective forms of instruction.

We call on **policymakers** to develop solutions that prioritize the acquisition and application of the science of reading in schools, and ensure that they are supported by realistic timelines and resources.

We call on **professional literacy associations** to provide learning opportunities and resources aligned to the science of reading.

We call on **reading scientists** to continue to investigate critical questions related to the science of reading, to translate important findings to practitioners in terminology that is readily applicable to their practice, and to actively seek outlets in which a direct partnership between scientists and educators can be developed.

We call on **parents and caregivers** to take an active part in ensuring schools and school systems are utilizing literacy practices aligned with the science of reading.

Being Good Citizens of a Science and Practice Community

- **Disagree respectfully**. Debate is a sign of a healthy scientific community. Science advances through questions and challenging previous conclusions. Acknowledge differences and discuss them with respect and decency.
- **Recognize the fallibility of anecdotes and personal experiences**. Our experiences were the product of the unique contexts in which they occurred. Personal experience and anecdotal observations should not outweigh findings of high-quality research.
- **Fairly evaluate all evidence**. Apply healthy critique to all studies, regardless of whether the conclusions are inconsistent with your beliefs.
- **Identify best practices from multiple studies**. Identifying "what works" comes from a body of high-quality studies.
- **Dig deeper and seek clarification**. Look closely at the sources that researchers, presenters, or program vendors cite as support. When needed, ask them for clarification.
- **Have courage to reconsider**. Be willing to change beliefs or practices in light of new evidence.
- **Self-critique**. Reflect on the ways you use and interpret evidence. Acknowledge when your understanding is incomplete, and invite feedback from others on your interpretation of research.
- **Examine and disclose conflicts of interest**. A researcher, presenter, or program developer should disclose when they profit from the use of a program or materials. A potential conflict of interest demands greater scrutiny of their claims.
- **Base decisions on quality of evidence, not popularity**. The popularity of an author or presenter should not be an indicator of the validity of their recommendations, nor should the popularity of a program be a reason to use it.

By Nathan Clemens (See Clemens, N.H., Powell, S.R., & Vaughn, S. (2021). A special educator's guide to evidence.)

In Conclusion: An Equity Statement

We believe that literacy success for all is the **defining human right** of the 21st century, regardless of zip code, ethnic origin, dialect, or language. We urge you to join us by insisting that all children are afforded instruction that prepares them to read and write at proficient and advanced levels. Children who are skilled readers and writers will be **empowered by their literacy** and will refuse to be defined by the low expectations of others.

We extend our deepest gratitude to the dedicated advocates of this Defining Movement. Together, we can elevate the stories of lives that have been dynamically altered through our **united commitment to improving literacy narratives using evidence-based practices**. Our children are worth the labor of pressing through the unknown, holding challenging conversations with high expectations, and even failing forward while building expertise.

Let us learn from the broken systems that have perpetuated unacceptable inequities, and forge ahead so that underserved families experience a **new social contract** that guarantees reading success for all. Families must be able to expect that when they send their children to school, they will learn to read at proficient and advanced levels.

Let us galvanize a critical mass of stakeholders who anchor their work in science through a commitment to deep, systemic, and non-negotiable transformation.

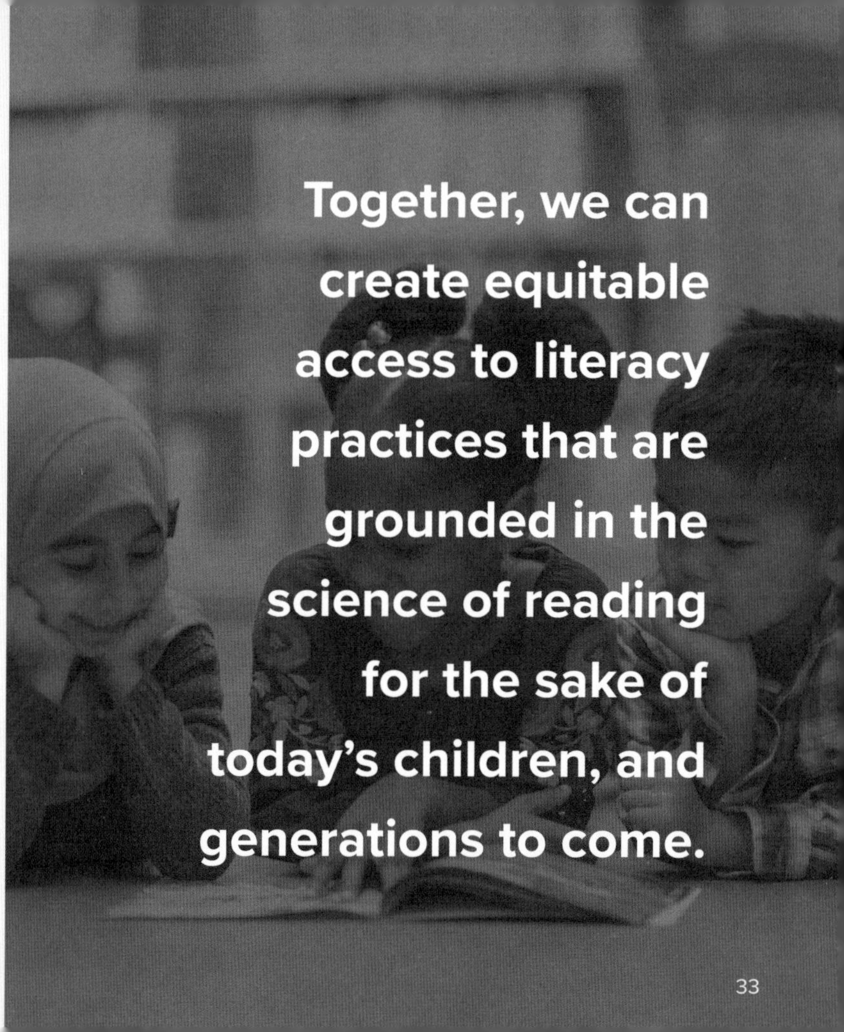

Together, we can create equitable access to literacy practices that are grounded in the science of reading for the sake of today's children, and generations to come.

The Defining Movement Coalition

The Defining Movement Coalition came together from September 2020 - July 2021 on a weekly basis to build the contents of this Defining Guide. The generosity they extended in terms of time and expertise stemmed from their desire to ensure that the findings from the science of reading are widely understood by all stakeholders. We hope this guide will assist practitioners and others to implement these findings in ways that will result in the same gap-closing outcomes so many scientific reading researchers achieved in their work.

Thank you to all. You are so valued.

Heidi Beverine-Curry, Ph.D., Chief Academic Officer, The Reading League

Kymyona Burk, Ed.D., Early Literacy Policy Director, Foundation for Excellence in Education

Kelly Butler, CEO, Barksdale Institute

Mary E. Dahlgren, Ed.D. President and Founder Tools 4 Reading

Linda Diamond, co-author "Teaching Reading Sourcebook" and "Assessing: Reading Multiple Measures" and Founder Consortium on Reaching Excellence in Education (CORE)

Melissa Farrall, Ph.D., Director for Evaluation, Stern Center for Language and Learning

Margie B. Gillis, Ed.D., Founder and President, Literacy How, Inc.

DeJunne' Clark Jackson, Vice President of Program Development, The Center for Literacy & Learning; Founder, Learning Fundamentals Educational Therapy & Consulting; President of The Reading League Louisiana; State Leader, Decoding Dyslexia Louisiana

Kelli Johnson, Director of Community Education and Engagement, The Reading League

Pam Kastner, Ed.D., State Lead Consultant for Literacy, The Pennsylvania Training and Technical Assistance Network (PaTTAN) & President of The Reading League Pennsylvania

Kari Kurto, Literacy Specialist, Rhode Island Department of Education

Amy McGovern, Reading Specialist & Associate Director of Continuous School Improvement Services at CESA 9, Vice President of The Reading League WI

Louisa C. Moats, Ed.D., President, Moats Associates Consulting, Inc., Sun Valley, Idaho

Maria Murray, Ph.D., President and CEO, The Reading League

Laura Stewart, Chief Innovation Officer, The Reading League

Stephanie A. Stollar, Ph.D., Part-Time Assistant Professor, Mount St. Joseph University, Founder of The Reading Science Academy

Pamela Toman, Co-Founder & Executive Director, TX Reads

Toni Ann Walsh, Chief Marketing and Development Officer, The Reading League

Dale W. Webster, Ph.D., Chief Academic Officer, Consortium on Reaching Excellence in Education (CORE)

Tracy Weeden, Ph.D., President and CEO, Neuhaus Education Center

Liz Woody-Remington, Co-Founder of The Learning Alliance and Director of Professional Development

THE READING LEAGUE

Sharing knowledge, inspiring change.

The Reading League is a national education nonprofit led by educators and reading experts dedicated to promoting knowledge that will accelerate the global movement toward evidence-aligned reading instruction.

We train and support educators and school leaders, and by extension, we also serve parents, specialists, and researchers. We believe all children deserve to learn to read and all teachers can learn to teach them.

thereadingleague.org

The Science of Reading

A Defining Movement

The Science of Reading: A Defining Movement was developed by The Reading League.

- All voices are needed to protect the science of reading.
- A worldwide commitment to understanding the science of reading ensures it is not misunderstood or minimally applied.

ACTION YOU CAN TAKE:

- Join our community
- Promote the science of reading in your work
- Share this book with colleagues

Scan for eBook and more information about the science of reading.

Use this space to define how you will commit to this movement: